I Wish I had a Mummy

This book is dedicated to the whole of my family,
especially my younger brother Thomas

I Wish I had a Mummy

by Bethan Sadler

Illustrated by Jan Lewis

First published in Great Britain by Heinemann Library,
Halley Court, Jordan Hill, Oxford OX2 8EJ
a division of Reed Educational and Professional Publishing Ltd.

Heinemann is a registered trademark of Reed Educational & Professional Publishing Limited.

OXFORD MELBOURNE AUCKLAND
IBADAN JOHANNESBURG GABORONE
PORTSMOUTH NH (USA) CHICAGO BLANTYRE

Designed by Joanna Hinton-Malivoire
Colour Reproduction by Dot Gradations Ltd
Printed and bound by Times Offset, Malaysia

02 01 00 99 98
10 9 8 7 6 5 4 3 2 1

British Library Cataloguing in Publication Data
Sadler, Bethan
   I wish I had a mummy. - (Get published)
   1. Children's stories
   I. Title
   823.9'14 [J]

ISBN 0 431 03428 1

The Heinemann Library GET PUBLISHED competition

For the second year running, this competition invited school children from all over the country to write a story book for 5 to 7 year olds. Over 6500 entries were sent in. Four winners were chosen from two age categories: 7-11 years and 12 plus. The winning authors have each had their book professionally edited, illustrated and marketed to schools and bookshops throughout the country, and will receive a royalty payment on their sales. Their schools also won £500 worth of books for their library.

The judges were:

Harriet Castor, author of *Fat Puss and Friends*
Jenni Murray, presenter of Woman's Hour on BBC Radio 4
Professor Ted Wragg, author and broadcaster
Jo Brown, Resource Librarian at Hertfordshire Schools Library Service
Nicole Irving, Commissioning Editor, Heinemann Library

The winning entries are:

Age 7–11
Willy the Wonderful Wishing Worm by Chris Schulz
Zit the Wish Bug by Philip Davison

Age 12 plus
Freddy's Wish by Karolina Edge
I Wish I had a Mummy by Bethan Sadler

You can read about the author and the illustrator of this book on the next page.

1996 winners:

The theme of the 1996 competition was 'Friends' and the four winners chosen from over 6000 entries were:
Ziggy the Alien by Hana Baig (0431 03421 4)
Giraffe in Distress by Emily Lines (0431 03422 2)
Ralph and Herman by Andrew James (0431 03420 6)
My First Day by Ashok Dhillon (0431 03423 0)

The author

Bethan Sadler was born in Hexham, Northumberland in 1985. She lived abroad in the Middle East and Japan from the age of one, and only returned to the UK in 1996. Bethan now attends Dr Challoners High School in Buckinghamshire. She plays the piano and cornet for pleasure and her current ambition is to be a doctor or a lawyer.

The illustrator

Jan Lewis studied illustration at Bath Academy of Art and has been illustrating since 1978 (and still loves it!). She now lives in Oxfordshire with her husband, Brian, and her two sons, Sam and Freddie. She is also kept very busy looking after her dog – Finlay, cat – Dave, parrot – Betty, and many, many chickens and ducks!

Cub was lonely. She had lots of friends, and
a lovely jungle to live in. But she did not have
a mummy. 'I wish I had a mummy,' Cub said.

'Will you be my mummy?' Cub asked the monkey.
'No,' said the monkey, 'you're too fierce to be my
child,' and with that, she darted up a tree.

'Will you be my mummy?' Cub asked the elephant.
'No,' he said, 'you are too small to be my child.'

'Will you be my mummy?' Cub asked the snake.
'No,' the snake hissed, 'you've got legs, ssso you
can't be my child,' and she slithered out of sight.

'Will you be my mummy?' Cub asked the frog. 'No,'
he croaked, 'your fur will be too soggy in the
water,' and the frog hopped away.

Cub squeezed under a bush...

... and she came nose to nose with a creature just like her! With black stripes, four legs, two brown eyes, and white whiskers. 'Will you be my mummy?'

Turn the page to see who will be Cub's mummy, then close the book, turn it upside down, and start again!

... and she came nose to nose with a small creature just like her! With black stripes, four legs, two brown eyes and white whiskers. 'Will you be my baby?'

Turn the page to see who will be Kara's baby, then close the book, turn it upside down, and start again!

Kara squeezed under a bush...

'Will you be my baby?' Kara asked the little frog.
'No!' he croaked, 'I already have a mummy.'

'Will you be my baby?' Kara asked the new-born snake. 'No,' she hissed softly, 'You look too ssstrong,' and she fell asleep.

'Will you be my baby?' Kara asked the baby elephant.
'No!' she said, 'You are too quick to be my mummy.'

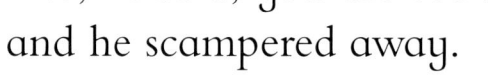

'Will you be my baby?' Kara asked the baby monkey.
'No,' he said, 'you are too scary to be my mummy,'
and he scampered away.

Kara was lonely. She had a warm soft bed, and a lovely home. But she did not have a baby. 'I wish I had a baby,' Kara said to herself.

This book is dedicated to the whole of my family,
especially my younger brother Thomas

I Wish I had a Baby

by Bethan Sadler

Illustrated by Jan Lewis

Heinemann
LIBRARY